The Gifts of Christmas

The Gifts of Christmas

by
Harold Ivan Smith

BEACON HILL PRESS OF KANSAS CITY
Kansas City, Missouri

Permission to quote from the following copyrighted versions is acknowledged with appreciation:

The Holy Bible, New International Version (NIV), copyright © 1973, 1978, 1984 by the International Bible Society.

The *Revised Standard Version of the Bible* (RSV), copyrighted 1946, 1952, © 1971, 1973 by the Division of Christian Education of the National Council of the Churches of Christ in the U.S.A.

KJV—King James Version

Unless otherwise indicated, all Scripture quotations are from the NIV.

10   9   8   7   6   5   4   3   2   1

Contents

The Gift in Scripture

Isaiah

SEE, THE SOVEREIGN LORD comes with power, and his arm rules for him. See, his reward is with him, and his recompense accompanies him.

He tends his flock like a shepherd: He gathers the lambs in his arms and carries them close to his heart; he gently leads those that have young. . . .

He grew up before him like a tender shoot, and like a root out of dry ground. He had no beauty or majesty to attract us to him, nothing in his appearance that we should desire him.

He was despised and rejected by men, a man of sorrows, and familiar with suffering. Like one from whom men hide their faces he was despised, and we esteemed him not.

Surely he took up our infirmities and carried our sorrows, yet we considered him stricken by God, smitten by him, and afflicted.

But he was pierced for our transgressions, he was crushed for our iniquities; the punishment that brought us peace was upon him, and by his wounds we are healed.

We all, like sheep, have gone astray, each of us has turned to his own way; and the Lord has laid on him the iniquity of us all.

He was oppressed and afflicted, yet he did not open his mouth; he was led like a lamb to the slaughter, and as a sheep before her shearers is silent, so he did not open his mouth.

—Isa. 40:10-11; 53:2-7

Micah

"BUT YOU, BETHLEHEM EPHRATHAH, though you are small among the clans of Judah, out of you will come for me one who will be ruler over Israel, whose origins are from of old, from ancient times." . . .

He will stand and shepherd his flock in the strength of the Lord, in the majesty of the name of the Lord his God. And they will live securely, for then his greatness will reach to the ends of the earth.

And he will be their peace.

—Mic. 5:2, 4-5

Matthew

THIS IS HOW THE BIRTH of Jesus Christ came about: His mother Mary was pledged to be married to Joseph, but before they came together, she was found to be with child through the Holy Spirit.

Because Joseph her husband was a righteous man and did not want to expose her to public disgrace, he had in mind to divorce her quietly.

But after he had considered this, an angel of the Lord appeared to him in a dream and said, "Joseph son of David, do not be afraid to take Mary home as your wife, because what is conceived in her is from the Holy Spirit.

She will give birth to a son, and you are to give him

the name Jesus, because he will save his people from their sins."

All this took place to fulfill what the Lord had said through the prophet:

"The virgin will be with child and will give birth to a son, and they will call him Immanuel"—which means, "God with us."

When Joseph woke up, he did what the angel of the Lord had commanded him and took Mary home as his wife.

But he had no union with her until she gave birth to a son. And he gave him the name Jesus.

—Matt. 1:18-25

Mary

IN THE SIXTH MONTH, God sent the angel Gabriel to Nazareth, a town in Galilee,

To a virgin pledged to be married to a man named Joseph, a descendant of David. The virgin's name was Mary.

The angel went to her and said, "Greetings, you who are highly favored! The Lord is with you."

Mary was greatly troubled at his words and wondered what kind of greeting this might be.

But the angel said to her, "Do not be afraid, Mary, you have found favor with God.

You will be with child and give birth to a son, and you are to give him the name Jesus.

He will be great and will be called the Son of the

Most High. The Lord God will give him the throne of his father David,

And he will reign over the house of Jacob forever; his kingdom will never end."

"How will this be," Mary asked the angel, "since I am a virgin?"

The angel answered, "The Holy Spirit will come upon you, and the power of the Most High will overshadow you. So the holy one to be born will be called the Son of God.

Even Elizabeth your relative is going to have a child in her old age, and she who was said to be barren is in her sixth month.

For nothing is impossible with God."

"I am the Lord's servant," Mary answered. "May it be to me as you have said." Then the angel left her.

And Mary said: "My soul glorifies the Lord and my spirit rejoices in God my Savior,

For he has been mindful of the humble state of his servant. From now on all generations will call me blessed,

For the Mighty One has done great things for me— holy is his name.

His mercy extends to those who fear him, from generation to generation.

He has performed mighty deeds with his arm; he has scattered those who are proud in their inmost thoughts.

He has brought down rulers from their thrones but has lifted up the humble.

He has filled the hungry with good things but has sent the rich away empty.

He has helped his servant Israel, remembering to be

merciful to Abraham and his descendants forever, even as he said to our fathers."

Mary stayed with Elizabeth for about three months and then returned home.

—Luke 1:26-38, 46-56

Elizabeth

AT THAT TIME MARY GOT READY and hurried to a town in the hill country of Judea,

Where she entered Zechariah's home and greeted Elizabeth.

When Elizabeth heard Mary's greeting, the baby leaped in her womb, and Elizabeth was filled with the Holy Spirit.

In a loud voice she exclaimed: "Blessed are you among women, and blessed is the child you will bear!

But why am I so favored, that the mother of my Lord should come to me?

As soon as the sound of your greeting reached my ears, the baby in my womb leaped for joy.

Blessed is she who has believed that what the Lord has said to her will be accomplished!"

—Luke 1:39-45

Zechariah

HIS FATHER ZECHARIAH was filled with the Holy Spirit and prophesied:

"Praise be to the Lord, the God of Israel, because he has come and has redeemed his people.

He has raised up a horn of salvation for us in the house of his servant David

(as he said through his holy prophets of long ago),

Salvation from our enemies and from the hand of all who hate us—

To show mercy to our fathers and to remember his holy covenant,

The oath he swore to our father Abraham:

To rescue us from the hand of our enemies, and to enable us to serve him without fear

In holiness and righteousness before him all our days.

And you, my child, will be called a prophet of the Most High; for you will go on before the Lord to prepare the way for him,

To give his people the knowledge of salvation through the forgiveness of their sins,

Because of the tender mercy of our God, by which the rising sun will come to us from heaven

To shine on those living in darkness and in the shadow of death, to guide our feet into the path of peace."

—Luke 1:67-79

Luke

IN THOSE DAYS CAESAR AUGUSTUS issued a decree that a census should be taken of the entire Roman world.

(This was the first census that took place while Quirinius was governor of Syria.)

And everyone went to his own town to register.

So Joseph also went up from the town of Nazareth in Galilee to Judea, to Bethlehem the town of David, because he belonged to the house and line of David.

He went there to register with Mary, who was pledged to be married to him and was expecting a child.

While they were there, the time came for the baby to be born,

And she gave birth to her firstborn, a son. She wrapped him in cloths and placed him in a manger, because there was no room for them in the inn.

—Luke 2:1-7

Shepherds and Angels

AND THERE WERE SHEPHERDS living out in the fields nearby, keeping watch over their flocks at night.

An angel of the Lord appeared to them, and the

glory of the Lord shone around them, and they were terrified.

But the angel said to them, "Do not be afraid. I bring you good news of great joy that will be for all the people.

Today in the town of David a Savior has been born to you; he is Christ the Lord.

This will be a sign to you: You will find a baby wrapped in cloths and lying in a manger."

Suddenly a great company of the heavenly host appeared with the angel, praising God and saying,

"Glory to God in the highest, and on earth peace to men on whom his favor rests."

When the angels had left them and gone into heaven, the shepherds said to one another, "Let's go to Bethlehem and see this thing that has happened, which the Lord has told us about."

So they hurried off and found Mary and Joseph, and the baby, who was lying in the manger.

When they had seen him, they spread the word concerning what had been told them about this child,

And all who heard it were amazed at what the shepherds said to them.

But Mary treasured up all these things and pondered them in her heart.

The shepherds returned, glorifying and praising God for all the things they had heard and seen, which were just as they had been told.

—Luke 2:8-20

Simeon

NOW THERE WAS A MAN in Jerusalem called Simeon, who was righteous and devout. He was waiting for the consolation of Israel, and the Holy Spirit was upon him.

It had been revealed to him by the Holy Spirit that he would not die before he had seen the Lord's Christ.

Moved by the Spirit, he went into the temple courts. When the parents brought in the child Jesus to do for him what the custom of the Law required,

Simeon took him in his arms and praised God, saying:

"Sovereign Lord, as you have promised, you now dismiss your servant in peace.

For my eyes have seen your salvation, which you have prepared in the sight of all people,

A light for revelation to the Gentiles and for glory to your people Israel."

The child's father and mother marveled at what was said about him.

Then Simeon blessed them and said to Mary, his mother: "This child is destined to cause the falling and rising of many in Israel, and to be a sign that will be spoken against,

So that the thoughts of many hearts will be revealed. And a sword will pierce your own soul too."

—Luke 2:25-35

Anna

THERE WAS ALSO A PROPHETESS, Anna, the daughter of Phanuel, of the tribe of Asher. She was very old; she had lived with her husband seven years after her marriage,

And then was a widow until she was eighty-four. She never left the temple but worshiped night and day, fasting and praying.

Coming up to them at that very moment, she gave thanks to God and spoke about the child to all who were looking forward to the redemption of Jerusalem.

—Luke 2:36-38

The Wise Men

AFTER JESUS WAS BORN in Bethlehem in Judea, during the time of King Herod, Magi from the east came to Jerusalem

And asked, "Where is the one who has been born king of the Jews? We saw his star in the east and have come to worship him."

When King Herod heard this he was disturbed, and all Jerusalem with him.

When he had called together all the people's chief priests and teachers of the law, he asked them where the Christ was to be born.

"In Bethlehem in Judea," they replied, "for this is what the prophet has written:

"'But you, Bethlehem, in the land of Judah, are by no means least among the rulers of Judah; for out of you will come a ruler who will be the shepherd of my people Israel.'"

Then Herod called the Magi secretly and found out from them the exact time the star had appeared.

He sent them to Bethlehem and said, "Go and make a careful search for the child. As soon as you find him, report to me, so that I too may go and worship him."

After they had heard the king, they went on their way, and the star they had seen in the east went ahead of them until it stopped over the place where the child was.

When they saw the star, they were overjoyed.

On coming to the house, they saw the child with his mother Mary, and they bowed down and worshiped him. Then they opened their treasures and presented him with gifts of gold and of incense and of myrrh.

And having been warned in a dream not to go back to Herod, they returned to their country by another route.

—Matt. 2:1-12

Jeremiah

WHEN THEY [THE MAGI] HAD GONE, an angel of the Lord appeared to Joseph in a dream. "Get up," he said, "take the child and his mother and escape to Egypt. Stay there until I tell you, for Herod is going to search for the child to kill him."

So he got up, took the child and his mother during the night and left for Egypt,

Where he stayed until the death of Herod. And so was fulfilled what the Lord had said through the prophet: "Out of Egypt I called my son."

When Herod realized that he had been outwitted by the Magi, he was furious, and he gave orders to kill all the boys in Bethlehem and its vicinity who were two years old and under, in accordance with the time he had learned from the Magi.

Then what was said through the prophet Jeremiah was fulfilled:

"A voice is heard in Ramah, weeping and great mourning, Rachel weeping for her children and refusing to be comforted, because they are no more."

—Matt. 2:13-18

John

IN THE BEGINNING WAS THE WORD, and the Word was with God, and the Word was God.

He was with God in the beginning.

Through him all things were made; without him nothing was made that has been made.

In him was life, and that life was the light of men.

The light shines in the darkness, but the darkness has not understood it. . . .

He was in the world, and though the world was made through him, the world did not recognize him.

He came to that which was his own, but his own did not receive him.

Yet to all who received him, to those who believed in his name, he gave the right to become children of God—

Children born not of natural descent, nor of human decision or a husband's will, but born of God.

The Word became flesh and made his dwelling among us. We have seen his glory, the glory of the One and Only, who came from the Father, full of grace and truth.

—John 1:1-5, 10-14

Paul

YOUR ATTITUDE SHOULD BE the same as that of Christ Jesus:

Who, being in very nature God, did not consider equality with God something to be grasped,

But made himself nothing, taking the very nature of a servant, being made in human likeness.

And being found in appearance as a man, he humbled himself and became obedient . . .

—Phil. 2:5-8

Thanks be to God for his indescribable gift!

—2 Cor. 9:15

Witnesses to the Gift

The Witness of Joseph:

A Model of Obedience

HE IS ONE OF THE FORGOTTEN MEN of the New Testament although he is essential for every Christmas pageant. After the holidays, he gets "put back on the shelf" until next year.

His name: Joseph; a carpenter, a Jew, a resident of a small town. Consider his problems: a pregnant fiancée, the growing escalation of Roman authority, a taxation, and census.

What characteristics did Joseph possess that merited his selection as the foster father of Jesus? Was his selection merely incidental, because he happened to be engaged to Mary? What characteristics would God consider essential in choosing two people who would create the home in which His Son would live? After all, Joseph and Mary had not already created that home.

Could God have trusted you with the custody of His Son?

How would you have responded? Joseph saw an opportunity for obedience in the complex situation he faced.

What do we know about Joseph the carpenter?

First, Joseph was "a righteous man" (Matt. 1:19). But surely there must have been thousands of equally righteous men who feared God, kept the Law, and could have acted responsibly. Yet Joseph was chosen.

Second, Joseph was not self-righteous. For some of his peers, righteousness had become a source of pride and spiritual blindness, especially for the Pharisees. If Joseph had been a legalist, he could have insisted on his rights as an offended groom when Mary "was found to be with child" (v. 18). Most men would have loudly wailed while demanding the penalty be paid in full!

Joseph may have pondered his rights, but he chose to think of Mary also. Anxious not to expose her publicly, he decided to divorce her privately in the presence of two witnesses, according to the custom of that day.

However, as a righteous man, it was natural that he should recognize God's voice in a dream. "Joseph son of David, do not be afraid to take Mary home as your wife, because what is conceived in her is from the Holy Spirit" (Matt. 1:20).

Third, Joseph was willing to be obedient. The angel instructed him in what were to be the first steps that tremendously complicated his life. Those directives led him away from the town he knew, away from business opportunities, first to Bethlehem, then to Egypt, and eventually back—a journey of obedience.

Why didn't the angel spell it all out for him in one dream? Or hand him a completed map and time schedule? Then Joseph could have fully understood the implications of his yes.

The first steps in obedience, perhaps exercised in faith, led to his confidence. God chose to unfold His will gradually to Joseph. He was not to divorce Mary; rather he was to marry her and assume parenthood for the Child she would bear.

The census complicated the issue. While he had to go to Bethlehem, the city of his ancestry, what was he to do with Mary, now well along in her pregnancy?

Thus the Roman intrusion became a surprise element in the journey of obedience as well as the fulfillment of prophecy. Perhaps Joseph had thought Bethlehem was to become their home.

Each directive or potential obstacle, although an imposition on the "rights" of Joseph, became another opportunity for obedience. Had Joseph known all the pieces of the puzzle, he might have worried or relied on his own understanding.

Because of his confidence, it was not all that difficult to hear the voice that awakened him in the night, saying, "Get up . . . take the child and his mother and escape to Egypt" (Matt. 2:13). Some might have responded, "OK, first thing in the morning." But not Joseph; he had learned the value of prompt obedience. He understood the vocal insistence: Now!

Later, in Egypt, another directive came from the angel to take the Child and return to the land of Israel. Yet another dream led him when he entered Israel and discovered Archelaus was reigning (v. 22).

Finally, Joseph was willing to let pieces remain unexplained. When he discovered that the Agent of the conception was the Holy Spirit, he did not demand an anatomical rationale. He accepted the Lord's intervention.

Perhaps you are requisitioning the details for the rest of your journey; you want the Lord to fill in the blanks, now. Before you act. Had Joseph been slow, disobedient, or impatient or had he demanded more details, history might have been altered. Perhaps Joseph could have sung with the songwriter:

> *He leadeth me! Oh, blessed tho't!*
> *Oh, words with heav'nly comfort fraught!*
> *Whate'er I do, where'er I be,*
> *Still 'tis God's hand that leadeth me.*
>
> *He leadeth me, He leadeth me.*
> *By His own hand He leadeth me.*
> *His faithful follower I would be,*
> *For by His hand He leadeth me.*

Apparently Joseph did not live to enjoy the luxury of his obedience: to see the Boy become a Man, to witness His ministry. Because Joseph is not mentioned in any of the later accounts of Jesus' family (Mark 6:3; Luke 8:19; John 2:12), his death is assumed by most scholars.

Surely, some of the qualities Jesus demonstrated were modeled by a man of obedience, Joseph, as they worked in the carpenter's shop.

Joseph, the supporting participant in the drama of Christmas, is a lesson not only to today's fathers but to tomorrow's fathers as well—a lesson of faithful obedience. There are times when we, too, must follow a step at a time, particularly as the opportunities for obedience that are part of our lives become apparent.

The obedience of Joseph is a courageous example for us. Joseph, stepfather to God's only Son, was found faithful. What a testimony! A man not only for the Christmas pageant, but a hero for Father's Day as well.

Dramatic Witness

BECAUSE MY FATHER was the church custodian when I was a boy, I became enormously interested in the annual Christmas pageants—"bathrobe dramas."

Every year near Christmas we began to plan for the production. The directors would always call on Dad to "make the scenery look realistic." So when we went to my grandfather's farm to cut down our Christmas tree, we also brought back a couple of other trees and some bales of hay for pageant atmosphere.

The night of the production, men in the church dressed in their bathrobes and disguised themselves with makeshift beards—really makeshift. Patronizing a theatre supply store was out of the question in my youth. It wasn't unusual for a fake beard to lose its mooring or the monk's cloth curtain to open too soon revealing a stage hand tinkering with the light bulb that represented the Christ child in the manger. But our actual performance was always greeted with hushed wonder and appreciative patience. Despite the clumsy presentation, the audience always marveled at the Christmas story.

After the curtain closed, our pastor would come and congratulate the cast, perhaps brag on a certain star performance, then bring out the director. It was the only time when applause was appropriate in our congregation.

An hour later, all the illusion and mystery were shattered when the bright fluorescent tubes flicked on, and a sanctuary covered with straw had to be cleaned up. Guess who got to do that? The Smith kids, that's who, while everyone else trooped downstairs for hot chocolate and glazed donuts.

Then one year the director decided to do a contemporary drama rather than the traditional wise-men-shepherds-angels-and-bales-of-hay production. The play was about a soldier who came home for Christmas and made life miserable for everyone. Since the teen group presented the play, there were only two parts for adults.

That year a lot of the men, who ordinarily had to be coaxed or coerced into playing wise men (and who seldom showed up for rehearsals and thereby raised the stress level of the pageant directors), breathed easier.

That was also the year I didn't get a part. Naturally, my feelings were hurt. After all, I was a member of the high school drama club. The previous Christmas I had been a shepherd and had delivered two well-enunciated lines. I'd assumed I would be promoted to a more significant role.

The next year I volunteered to direct the Christmas play. The pastor thought it was a great idea, since that meant his wife would not have to do it.

So we presented my version of the Christmas pageant. Since I had the power of director, I used it like a show biz mogul. Those who had had the star roles the previous year were relegated to the very back row of the host of angels.

That all seems terribly silly now. Yet across these years I have maintained an interest in church dramas. There is something about the Christmas story that stimulates my creative juices and brings out my best bathrobe instincts.

In one sense, if you have seen one such drama you have seen them all—unless you remember the year Brother Baker played the prophet because he looked the part. But his work schedule necessitated that he miss all of the rehearsals, with him insisting that he had his lines down cold.

The result was in that dramatic moment when he was centerstage with Mary and Joseph, he forgot his lines.

However, in a flash of inspiration, he began sharing his salvation experience from World War II, or "the Big One," as he called it.

The director survived her near cardiac arrest only after someone had the insight to use the shepherd's crook for more than a prop. I can still hear his "but I'm not through" as he was slowly pulled off stage. Quite a moment!

Most of the dramas I've seen have gone more smoothly. They stick to the main cast of characters and tell the Christmas story in a very traditional way. But there is probably a sense in which playwrights have focused too narrowly on Matt. 1:18—2:12 and Luke 2:1-20. There's more to the story!

On the eighth day, when it was time to circumcise him, he was named Jesus, the name the angel had given him before he had been conceived.

When the time of their purification according to the Law of Moses had been completed, Joseph and Mary took him to Jerusalem to present him to the Lord (as it is written in the Law of the Lord, "Every firstborn male is to be consecrated to the Lord"), and to offer a sacrifice in keeping with what is said in the Law of the Lord: "a pair of doves or two young pigeons."

Now there was a man in Jerusalem called Simeon, who was righteous and devout. He was waiting for the consolation of Israel, and the Holy Spirit was upon him. It had been revealed to him by the Holy Spirit that he would not die before he had seen the Lord's Christ. Moved by the Spirit, he went into the temple courts. When the parents brought in the child Jesus to do for him what the custom of the Law required, Simeon took him in his arms and praised God, saying:

"Sovereign Lord, as you have promised,
    you now dismiss your servant in peace.
For my eyes have seen your salvation,
    which you have prepared in the sight
    of all people,
a light for revelation to the Gentiles
    and for glory to your people Israel."

The child's father and mother marveled at what was said about him. Then Simeon blessed them and said to Mary, his mother: "This child is destined to cause the falling and rising of many in Israel, and to be a sign that will be spoken against, so that the thoughts of many hearts will be revealed. And a sword will pierce your own soul too."

There was also a prophetess, Anna, the daughter of Phanuel, of the tribe of Asher. She was very old; she had lived with her husband seven years after her marriage, and then was a widow until she was eighty-four. She never left the temple but worshiped night and day, fasting and praying. Coming up to them at that very moment, she gave thanks to God and

spoke about the child to all who were looking
forward to the redemption of Jerusalem.

LUKE 2:21-38

It seems to me there are two key witnesses who
have been overlooked or ignored—because there's only
so much time to do a pageant. The forgotten are:

- the witness of Simeon
- the witness of Anna

Both have great significance. Of course, Brother
Baker realized that.

The Witness of Simeon

NEARLY SIX WEEKS, 40 days, passed from Christ's birth until Mary and Joseph went to the Temple in Jerusalem for two important rites: (1) to redeem the firstborn; and (2) to purify Mary. The Law had to be satisfied even for Bethlehem's Babe.

When a male was born, the mother was considered ceremonially unclean or defiled for seven days preceding the child's circumcision. For another 33 days, she was still unclean and could not touch anything sacred or enter the Temple. (If the child was female, the uncleanness lasted twice as long.)

Someone observed, "The Lord must have loved poor people, He made so many of them." It's too bad some of the so-called prosperity prophets weren't around then. I wonder how they would explain this passage: Mary and Joseph were poor. And not because they didn't have faith. They would never have been chosen as parents if that vital ingredient had been missing.

As Mary and Joseph journeyed to Jerusalem to fulfill the rites, there in the Temple, a man waited. Not just any man, but a righteous and devout man who waited for the consolation of Israel—the fulfillment of the Messianic dreams (Luke 2:25). As he waited, "the Holy Spirit was upon him." Waiting seems to be a frequent requirement for blessing. In Acts, the apostles waited in Jerusalem "for the gift my Father promised" (Acts 1:4), for the Holy Spirit.

How long had Simeon been waiting? We don't know. From God's perspective, waiting is never measured in seconds, minutes, hours, days, weeks, months, or even years. It does not matter how long Simeon had been waiting, but only that he had been obediently waiting.

How incredible his waiting seems to those of us who are members of an impatient generation. We've all seen that cartoon that says, "You want it *when?*" We expect instant television, instant coffee, and instant credit.

We don't wait well. Isaiah reminds us of the value of waiting: "They who wait for the Lord shall renew their strength, they shall mount up with wings like eagles, they shall run and not be weary, they shall walk and not faint" (Isa. 40:31, RSV). He concludes, "Blessed are all who wait for him!" (30:18).

I suspect, it was not hard for Simeon to wait. After all, he knew that "he would not die before he had seen the Lord's Christ" (Luke 2:26). We have heard stories of someone who died after a long-awaited event, perhaps the birth of a grandchild. Simeon waited for the Gift Child.

As he waited, he may have remembered God's words to Habakkuk, "Write down the revelation and make it plain on tablets . . . For the revelation awaits an appointed time; it speaks of the end and will not prove false. Though it linger," Habakkuk was told, don't get impatient (he had only to think of Saul's tragic impatience [1 Sam. 13:5-14]). "Wait for it, it will certainly come and will not delay" (Hab. 2:2-3).

Now, "moved by the Spirit" (Luke 2:27), Simeon "went into the temple courts." This was probably his daily routine or habit. Did he suspect that *this* day, this particular act of obedience would be any different? Probably not; he simply obeyed.

Mary and Joseph and the Baby entered the Temple. What an intersection! Some of us would have perhaps been too busy, even though devout and religious, to have noticed these parents. Dietrich Bonhoeffer warned, "We must be ready to allow ourselves to be interrupted by God. God will be constantly crossing our paths and canceling our plans by sending up people with claims and petitions."[1]

Wham! The great moment for which Simeon had waited unfolded. Certainly he had seen other babies presented. So what made this One different? "Moved by the Spirit," Simeon knew.

Simeon took the Babe in his arms and praised God (v. 28). He spoke, no doubt slowly, through tears, through joy, over a pounding heart, with incredible conviction. His response differs from that of the wise men. For some reason Luke reports no verbatim dialogue of their visit. Matthew notes, "On coming to the house, they saw the child with his mother Mary, and they bowed down and worshiped him. Then they opened their treasures and presented him with gifts" (2:11).

The shepherds had only the time from the arrival of the angel band until their arrival at the manger to compose their praise song, though later they "spread the word" and were "glorifying and praising God" (Luke 2:17, 20). The wise men had the time from when they first spotted the star, trekked across the sands, and arrived at Bethlehem's house, to compose their song.

But Simeon had been composing for a longer time. Now, moved by the Spirit, he spoke. Peter later explained, "Prophecy never had its origin in the will of man, but men spoke from God as they were carried along by the Holy Spirit" (2 Pet. 1:21).

Simeon prayed: "Sovereign Lord, as you have promised, you now dismiss your servant in peace. For my eyes have seen your salvation, which you have prepared in the sight of all people, a light for revelation to the Gentiles and for glory to your people Israel" (Luke 2:29-32).

There are two key ideas in Simeon's prophecy. He called the Baby:

- a light for revelation to the Gentiles—that's us
- light for glory to Israel.

A father may be expected to boast about his children, but the greatness of Jesus was predicted by one who was a total stranger to Mary and Joseph.

However, the prophet didn't finish at foretelling Jesus' greatness. Simeon had tough words he *must* deliver. *"This child is destined to cause the falling and rising of many in Israel,"* he said (Luke 2:34). That was rooted in Isaiah's prophecy: "For both houses of Israel he will be a stone that causes men to stumble and a rock that makes them fall" (8:14).

Although Jesus was later called "the Cornerstone," first He would be a stumbling block (1 Pet. 2:6-8).

Until this point, we have been simply admiring a baby. As Walter Russell Bowie noted: "Anyone who had happened along the street of Bethlehem might have looked good-naturedly at the Baby lying in Mary's arms, but by no means everybody would have looked good-naturedly at the Son of Man who afterward went out of Nazareth."[2]

Ironically, perhaps some of those people who exclaimed over Mary's Baby in the streets of Jerusalem later screamed for Jesus' death.

"To be a sign that will be spoken against" (Luke 2:34). Simeon surely spoke accurately concerning Christ:

- His works were attributed to Satan.
- His deity was challenged.
- His motives were impugned.
- His cross would be a stigma.

Because of His ministry, *"the thoughts of many hearts will be revealed"* (Luke 2:35). Mary and Joseph must have been shaken by this point. Men of God, like Simeon, dared not edit even one word. Jeremiah had been com-

manded, "Speak to all the people . . . Tell them everything I command you; do not omit a word" (Jer. 26:2).

Prophets have spent an apprenticeship in obedience.

Simeon is merely following orders when he says,
"And a sword will pierce your own soul too" (Luke 2:35).

His words are directed to Mary. After this occasion
and the experience of losing Jesus in the Temple 12
years later, Joseph fades. Many scholars assume he died;
thus, Mary spent many years as a widow. As her firstborn, Jesus would then have assumed the responsibility
for her.

Whatever the reason, the conspicuous silence about
Joseph is significant for a male-dominated society. Re-
call Jesus' last words from the Cross to John, "Behold,
your mother!" (John 19:27, RSV).

Consider the mental and emotional wallop of Simeon's pronouncements. In Luke 1, when the birth of
Jesus had been foretold, the angel had said, "Greetings,
you who are highly favored! The Lord is with you" (v.
28). There was no mention of a sword, of suffering. Simeon seemingly contradicts the joy of the angel's procla-
mation by prophesying, "A sword is going to pierce
your heart!"

That's like rain on a parade. Perhaps Mary protested, "But the angel said, '. . . favored . . .'"

Mary had to balance Simeon's words with those of
the angel: "Do not be afraid . . . [the] son . . . will be great
and will be called the Son of the Most High. The Lord
God will give him the throne of his father David, and
he will reign . . . forever; his kingdom will never end"
(1:30-33).

All that with the light accompaniment of the angelic band. Who was Mary to believe?

Simeon was saying something quite different:

- He is destined to cause the falling . . . of many in Israel.
- He is destined to be a sign spoken against.
- He is destined to be a revealer of hearts.
- He is destined to be a soul-piercer.

He could fulfill the angel's words only by breaking Mary's heart.

Simeon spoiled the whole occasion for Mary and Joseph with the gravity of His words. In the middle of their celebration, the bubble got popped.

But God wasn't insensitive. A second witness waited.

The Witness
of Anna

S IMEON WASN'T THE ONLY PERSON WAITING. In this
story we have Simeon *and* Anna, a man and a
woman. In a time of darkness and great spiritual leth-
argy, God seldom has Lone Rangers.

Anna, too, was waiting. Scholars disagree on her
age. However, they agree that:

- She had married young.
- She had lived with her husband seven years.
- Then she became a widow and spent her time in
  the Temple.

Luke 2:37 in the NIV reads "until she was eighty-
four"; most other translations agree, though a few state
(or imply) she was "a widow for eighty-four years." Ei-
ther way, she was old by the life expectancy charts of
that day. As a single person, she had plenty of time to
devote to her waiting. Luke described her life-style: "She
never left the temple but worshiped night and day, fasting and praying" (2:37).

Anna offers guidelines for today's single adult
waiting for Prince or Princess Charming to show up.
Anna chose to seek the kingdom of God.

- *Anna never left the Temple.* She kept herself in a
place where she could wait for God.

- *Anna worshiped night and day.* That she had not
remarried was perceived as a virtue. Her example was
not forgotten. Perhaps Anna was Paul's model when he
advised the Early Church in formulating a policy on the
care of widows: "The widow who is really in need and
left all alone puts her hope in God and continues *night*

and day to pray and to ask God for help. But the widow who lives for pleasure is dead even while she lives" (1 Tim. 5:5-6, italics added).

And that night season means loneliness! Today we often sing an old gospel song with the words "God leads His dear children along . . . *In the night season* and all the day long" (italics added).

This emphasis seems strange to us, but not to a Jew of that day, whose day began at sundown. Consider Gen. 1:5: "And there was evening, and there was morning—the first day." The sequence continues in verses 8, 13, 19, 23, 31 and in some of our lives, where evening or darkness predominates.

Imagine how it must have been for Anna: no AM/FM radio, no Carson or Ted Koppel on "Nightline," no Larry King talk shows, no all-night coffee shops or doughnut emporiums.

So what did she do all evening long? She worshiped (Luke 2:37).

● *Anna fasted.* Though perhaps she didn't have much money, she knew that even good Jews were only expected to fast one day a week. But she also knew the spiritual value of abstaining from food in order to draw nearer to God.

● *Anna prayed.* I believe that as a result of her commitment to pray, she was "coming up to them *at that very moment*" (v. 38, italics added).

What moment: The moment Simeon was delivering his tough words.

● *Anna gave thanks to God* for allowing her to live long enough to see this child. That's natural because thanksgiving had been the agenda of her life for most of her long years.

Anna was a worshiper, a waiter. And the Lord rewarded her effort and her faithfulness by allowing her to be part of the ritual of presenting the child. Remember Isaiah's words:

"To the eunuchs who keep my Sabbaths,
- who choose what pleases me
- and hold fast to my covenant—*to them* I will give within my temple and its walls
- a memorial and a name
- better than sons and daughters;
I will give them an everlasting name
- that will not be cut off" (Isa. 56:4-5, italics added).

Possibly you flinched at the word *eunuch*. We generally associate that word with castration. Donald Goergin, along with many other respected scholars, insists our understanding is too narrow. Goergin argues that the word includes those who are celibate by choice as well as by surgical means.[3]

Whatever the meaning of the word, God fulfilled Isaiah's promise, because we know Anna's name. For some reason we are also given something of her family tree, although nothing is revealed about Simeon's. Let me illustrate how her name proves God's promise.

For one thing, can you name your great-great-grandmother? (You have eight to choose from.) Probably not, unless you are into genealogy. Yet we remember a widow by name from 2,000 years ago. How many have named daughters after this waiter? God is able to deliver on promises . . . then *and now.*

Second, we should note the fulfillment of prophecy. Simeon's words demonstrate that even in the first days after Jesus' birth, God was not content for people merely to ogle the Baby! From the first moment Jesus came He had a destiny, an appointment. It is ironic that both the crib and the Cross were made from the same material. Simeon boldly declared the Babe's destiny.

We also need to consider this as the initiation of Joel's prophecy: "I will pour out my Spirit on *all* people. Your sons *and daughters* will prophesy, your old men will dream dreams, your young men will see visions. Even on my servants, both men *and women*, I will pour out my Spirit in those days" (2:28-29, italics added).

This is a foretaste of what is to come: Not only is Mary to be a heroine, but so is Anna. God deliberately chose another woman to comfort Mary's troubled heart. But it didn't stop there—Anna became the first woman evangelist. "She . . . spoke about the child," Luke records, *"to all* who were looking forward to the redemption of Jerusalem" (2:38, italics added).

Consider the consequences of this meeting. For Simeon it was a benediction: "As you have promised, you now dismiss your servant in peace" (v. 29). Simeon had a destination, but Anna had an assignment. The Child recharged the widow's faithfulness.

Many single persons are tempted to ignore Christmas, but the very presence of Anna in the Christmas story, although neglected in the pageants and carols, can reaffirm their faith. God *deliberately* chose to include one who had been excluded under the family emphasis of the Jews.

Jesus would later say, "The Spirit of the Lord is on me, because he has anointed me to preach good news to the poor. He has sent me to proclaim freedom for the prisoners and recovery of sight for the blind, to release the oppressed, to proclaim [to all] the year of the Lord's favor" (Luke 4:18-19).

Obedience always pays great dividends. God rewards those who wait. When Simeon and Anna woke up that morning, did they have any indication that the day was to be different: Or were they simply in the habit of obeying all the time—not just on this day? of trusting and obeying?

Anna and Simeon were included in the scriptural accounts because both were in a place where they could respond to the Spirit's promptings.

If I could ask them one question, I would want to know: "Was it worth the wait?"

I think they would answer yes.

If the witnesses of Anna and Simeon were deemed significant enough by the Holy Spirit in His inspiration of Luke to ensure their inclusion in Scripture, how can we possibly overlook them in our Christmas pageants and carols?

My question is: *Are you in a place where you can easily respond to the Spirit's prompting?*

- Are you available for God to use you?
- What are you waiting for?
- Are you fasting?
- Are you praying?
- Are you worshiping night and day?

Gifts for the Hurting

Let There Be Peace on Earth!

ET THERE BE PEACE ON EARTH!" That's what the wrapping paper said in bold yet tasteful letters. The paper's texture, message, and design—and price— had caught my eye. So I bought two rolls, anticipating my wrapping paper needs for the Christmas season.

When I found myself needing wrapping paper in July, I resorted reluctantly to the leftover Christmas wrap. Why not have "peace on earth" at times other than Christmas? Why not have some Christmas carols in July or April?

"Blessed are the peacemakers"—Jesus' words (Matt. 5:9). Good words, words my mother used to settle neighborhood fights between preadolescent boys (including her sons). "You be the peacemaker!"

I remembered her words when I read the news reports on the crash of a chartered jet in Gander, New-foundland, that killed 256 people. Most of them were American soldiers returning from—you guessed— peacekeeping duty in the Middle East.

The pictures of the wreckage and of the memorial service in Clarksville, Tenn., remind me of the tentativeness of life. No doubt when they kissed wives, mothers, and girlfriends before heading off to the unstable Middle East, there was apprehension. "But we're just peacekeepers," they surely argued.

Yet they did not die like the Marines at the U.S. embassy in Lebanon. They died on the way home. Who would have thought Gander, Newfoundland, could be terminal?

Just minutes before takeoff in Gander, those soldiers had laughed and sung and bought souvenirs in airport shops. An hour later, their bodies were strewn through the trees nearby.

Clearly, this group of courageous peacemakers must have thought they had been "blessed" to get to go home for Christmas. But that's not the way it ended.

"Blessed are the peacemakers," huh? Why can't there be "peace on earth"? Why can't there be a cease-fire for the month of December? Why can't December have some mystic potential to alter our realities?

Ironically, it was a small article that hurt me most, "Claims by Two Groups Discounted." I read, "Two Middle East groups have claimed responsibility for the crash." One group, calling itself the Islamic Holy War, and another, the Organization for the Liberation of Egypt, both called news agencies to report responsibility. (Neither admitted cooperation with the other.)

Why? Why would someone want to claim 256 lives? Just another evidence of the validity of the carol's lyrics, "for hate is strong, and mocks the song of peace on earth, goodwill to men."

In researching this project, I decided to read Christmas editorials from magazines published during World War II. I found this editor's words as valid today as in 1944, when he wrote: "What more meaningful message could be proclaimed to a world given to fighting, driven mad by hate, bent on devastation, destruction, and death, and filled with suspicion and distrust—our world—than the old, old Christmas message that God loves and cares for the world."[1]

"Let there be peace on earth." Whether with or without the exclamation mark, whether a shout or a mumble, let it be our heart cry this Christmas season.

The Gift
of Presence

PRESENTS SEEM TO BE increasingly important to the mood of Christmas. So many—family, friends, colleagues—to buy for, and not just anything will do. Then there are those who merit special planning and scheming.

Sometime during Advent it becomes necessary to take a time-out from the busyness of Christmas: one too many parties, one too many presents to buy, one too many responsibilities. There are persons who discover in January they have missed Christmas again.

Others chase the season with a scowl. They plow through Christmas with mechanical devotion to details and set rigid limits on their giving ($5.00—not a penny more—for Mrs. Snyder's present). A few walk through Christmas as if on eggshells, folding their arms to protect themselves from the intrusion of overly zealous enjoyers of Christmas.

Yet there are those who wander through Advent with a sense of wonder and delight. Some listen to the carols, gaze in every window, smile at even the most harried clerk. They go through the season with arms wide open, giving of themselves, fully eager to experience the season.

Children learn early the significance of the wise men; they brought gifts: gold, frankincense, and myrrh, although we do not know for certain what Mary and Joseph did with them. Somehow, many have concluded that the presents of the wise men is a rationale for our riotous Christmas spending. We overlook the participation of "certain poor shepherds," in the words of the carol.

Luke reported, "There were shepherds living out in the fields nearby, keeping watch over their flocks" (2:8). We do not know whether they were "all seated on the ground," as another carol suggests.

The angel that appeared brought "good news of great joy"—a Savior had been born. If that were not dramatic enough, a multitude of angels appeared and began singing.

A close reading of the passage reveals that the angel did not specifically invite the shepherds but offered a clue to the whereabouts of the Child: "You will find a baby wrapped in cloths and lying in a manger" (v. 12).

The thought came to some shepherd, "Wow, I'd sure like to see that!" But how would it sound to the others? Leave the sheep to go look at a baby! They would howl.

Apparently the thought was shared by several shepherds. They concluded, "Let's go to Bethlehem and see this thing that has happened, which the Lord has told us about" (v. 15).

What was the significance of the shepherds' visit?

1. The good news was "for all the people" (v. 10). The shepherds represented the poor, the common people of earth. They, too, would be impacted by this momentous birth.

2. The shepherds represented a symbolic tie with the lineage of Jesus and portrayed His future as "great Shepherd" (Heb. 13:20).

Who has not marveled at Handel's aria for altos, part of the *Messiah:* "He shall feed his flock like a shepherd . . ." (Isa. 40:11, KJV). Jesus would acknowledge His role: "I am the good shepherd; I know my sheep and my sheep know me" (John 10:14).

3. The shepherds offered themselves; it's probably all they had. They gave presence rather than presents, a

truth we too must consider. "In my hand no price I bring. Simply to Thy cross I cling."

The stable must have been somewhat less idyllic than the poets, scholars, artists, and preachers have suggested. Consider the young couple at such a meaningful moment, away from the comforts of the familiar and family. There is a beauty of sharing a baby's birth with others. Why else do we hurry to the hospital to see the new mother and child? What if the shepherds had stayed home?

The real gift of presence was extravagant. Many would have said, "You didn't have to do that, to give Your only Son." But God did. What if He had only sent His Son for a month or a year at most? Since He had to die, it matters that He was of full age—around 33. Jesus could not have atoned for us in death in a Bethlehem manger, but rather on a cross at Calvary.

It was also a question of exposure, of willingness. The only way He could fully understand us was to come and live among us. The only way He could redeem us was to die for us. He did not come to run a limited race: "I'll give this much and see if it is enough." He gave fully.

He gave without reservation and without condemnation. His death was not to create an ultimate guilt trip that would force us to come to Him. It was to offer a path to eternal life through Him. "For God did not send his Son into the world to condemn the world, but to save the world through him" (John 3:17). How many times has John 3:16 been quoted with an attitude that contradicts verse 17?

Christ's gift was complete. He gave all; not in stages, measured and calculated to see what would be sufficient. He gave all, once and for all. Yet look how grudgingly many celebrate His birth!

Presence. God knew that the immediate family of

Mary and Joseph could not be with them, so He invited others. After all, the writer of Proverbs had observed, "Better a neighbor nearby than a brother far away" (27:10). And this departure from the narrow definitions of Jewish family to the broader parameters of Christian family has meaning for us.

"Oh, there's no place like home for the holidays" is a nostalgic song of the season. Christmas is said to be a "family time." Yet some families are estranged by design, others by distance. How many families would opt for presence rather than presents? "At least we're all together."

A friend of mine has custody of his two sons after an unpleasant divorce. The first Christmas after the divorce, the boys spent the weekend before Christmas with their mother. They returned to the father, laden with expensive gifts, toys, and clothes. Carefully they announced the significance of each gift. "Look what Mom got us . . . Look what Grandma bought us." Then they turned to a rather barren Christmas tree and asked, "Dad, what are you going to give us?" The situation offered an opportunity to "one-up" the mother. The implication was, "You've got to top this."

John sat his boys in the middle of the bounty scattered on the living room floor. He searched for the right words. How could they understand the background for this awkward moment?

"Boys, the only thing I have to give you is myself. That's not much, but it is all I have to give. I promise I'll never leave you. I'll always try to be here when you need me, in July as well as at Christmas." He paused for a moment. "Now, what more do you want?"

He was not being egotistical—just honest. He had little to give materially. After a moment of silence, the boys climbed over the loot and threw their arms around their dad.

"We love you, Daddy. You're all we want." John's arms reached out and pulled the two boys close. He did not have to run down their mother or commit himself to a Christmas that would leave him financially strapped the rest of the year. He gave himself.

Mary and Joseph opened their stable home to the shepherds. Perhaps that could be an example to us this Christmas. During this season, are there new people or lonely people in your congregation you could invite to share some time around your Advent hearth?

I learned a new tradition from my major professor in graduate school. She had no family, so her host of students and colleagues became family. Each person who came to her open house received a small white card attached to a colorful ribbon. They were asked to sign their names and write out a Christmas message. Then they hung the card on the tree.

New Year's Day, when the tree came down, she reviewed the cards. She was always amazed at how many new friends she had made since the previous Christmas.

Maybe it's a nursing home or hospital or jail that needs your Christmas presence.

In the light of our Lord's example and sacrifice, the right question at Christmas is not, "What are you going to give us?" but, "What can we give you?" In a season that focuses on gifts that can be unwrapped, there is the marvelous gift of presence that can be equally valued.

How to Help the Hurting

HOLIDAYS ARE FAMILY TIMES. Just listen to the commercials, notice the ads. But for some, Christmas is a quiet season, not because they don't know the Christ of Christmas, but because someone with whom they have shared previous Christmas seasons is absent— through death, divorce, or separation.

Take Ken and Beth. Everyone had expected a first Christmas for a new little Anderson. The previous holiday season, the young couple had openly talked about starting a family. But then the unthinkable happened— divorce.

Although Ken's family went out of the way to ignore their own hurt, Beth's absence was conspicuous. "Someone say something!" seemed to be on each family member's mind. They figuratively tiptoed around Ken, lest someone mention Beth's name.

Finally a niece, too young to understand, spilled the beans to the horror of all: "Where's Aunt Beth?" The question was ignored; the subject quickly changed. Grandmother whisked her away for a cookie.

Another family experienced their first Christmas without a family member—a son and husband—who had died. The emotions were similar.

In other families, some deviation from the traditional has tarnished the Christmas mood. This past year my married brother missed his first Christmas Eve with our family in 17 years, due to illness. As much as we tried, it wasn't the same.

How do you handle the absence of a loved one? Here are a few helpful guidelines.

1. If you adopt a "Don't mention his name" rule, you'll make conversation strained and unnatural. When relatives spend time trying not to mention a person, the conversation becomes mechanical and stilted. Open up and talk.

2. Consider a new time or location for your family celebration. Maybe this is the year to celebrate on Christmas Eve rather than on the morning of the 25th. Perhaps a meal in a restaurant or another family member's home would be better than the traditional time and locale.

3. If you keep old traditions, give the grieving an opportunity to say no or limit their involvement. Don't wait until the day before the event to ask their intentions. They may need to know that you still want them to participate. The Christmas blues are real. The wounded may feel further alienated because everyone is having a good time; or they may feel guilty that they are putting a brake on the celebration. Others may wish to withdraw into a cocoon and await the new year.

4. Don't insist old traditions be completed. When they produce a flood of discomfort or stress, they are counterproductive. Give a person a graceful way—even at the last moment—to take a time-out or say, "I'd better pass."

In my family, we gathered at my sister's home to open presents on Christmas Eve. My parents went early to handle the last-minute details involved in the orchestration of such a gathering. As a newly divorced person, I chose to drive so I could leave when I felt the need rather than impose my discomfort upon them.

That evening, I went through the routines and used some "canned" laughter and Christmas enthusiasm, but I did make it through the evening. The next morning, I was glad I had attempted the traditional Christmas Eve with my family.

5. Be cautious about dismissing a loved one's feelings. Don't manipulate someone into celebrating: "If you're not here, it just won't be the same." Or, "I won't hear of you spending Christmas alone!"

Be aware that a few have a strange need to be punished for what they've done (this is especially true for the initiators of divorce): "I don't deserve to enjoy Christmas."

6. Be prepared to offer a chance to reconsider. Many will appreciate an opportunity to change their minds: "You know, I've been thinking . . . and if your offer still stands, I'd like to take you up on it." Be willing to be inconvenienced again if you've already made one change of plans at their request.

7. Watch how you react. It is important. Try not to be too disappointed if they are quiet participants in the season.

Realize that some people need selective aloneness. They may be willing to spend some time with you but may not be excited about wall-to-wall people (who probably will have questions).

8. Do not try to make it up to the bereaved or divorced economically. And the grieving should realize that they can wreak havoc with "plastic money." If they gave generously last year, they may feel obligated to use credit cards to bolster their wounded egos. After all, what kind of person would neglect family or parents?

So the divorced, already threatened with the loss of self-worth, may go overboard, using gift giving as an anesthetic to dull their own pain or the discomfort they have caused others.

Confronting the bittersweet memories is difficult for all. To avoid the moment or to postpone it forever is to deny reality. And sometimes, through tears, the grieving must say as sad a "good-bye" to traditions as they have to the people with whom they shared those moments.

Distracted by All the Preparations?

CHRISTMAS IS A GREAT TIME for planting seeds in our memories that will bloom on a rainy afternoon, on a lonely evening, or at dawn after a night of little sleep. What would Christmas be without Kodak or Polaroid? Christmas is sights, sounds, smells, and sensitivity.

For many, though, Christmas is a time of anxiety. Too many decisions must be made about color, size, appropriateness, and cost. Every year adds complications. One reason many insist on knowing how many days are left until Christmas is subliminal: How many days until it's over?

Two sisters were excited about an open house they were having for an admired friend. Everything had to be just right for the guest: menu, appetizers, cleaning, baking. Each sister had a clear understanding of her duties so that the evening would go as planned.

When the guest of honor arrived, one sister forgot her assignments and became absorbed with the guest. Her sister, "distracted by all the preparations," tried everything to gain her attention; she cleared her throat, made subtle hints. Finally, in desperation, realizing her sister was not going to budge, she decided to embarrass her. She approached the guest. "Don't you care that my sister has left me to do the work by myself? Tell her to help me!" (Luke 10:40).

What was Jesus to do? Here were Mary and Martha, tense and at odds. Jesus could not say, "Mary, go help your sister, there's always time to listen to Me." Yet

He realized Martha's need that everything go as planned.

Too often, Christmas hospitality becomes a chore or a burden. Simple meals become complicated. The search for something different or special sends cooks to survey cookbooks for the right recipe. In the midst of the preparations a mother says, "Can't you see I'm busy!" or "I just don't have time!" For the moment, the cookie becomes more important than the child who will eat it.

Some become involved in pageants, plays, and cantatas to make the Christmas season more meaningful to others. But in the quiet of the spirit comes the question, "Who is going to make it meaningful for me?"

The patience of even seasoned play directors and music ministers can be quickly strained during the season. Why is it that when you need to rehearse the three wise men for their grand entrance, or the soprano for the solo, they cannot be there "until later?" How many secretly long for it to be all over so they can relax and enjoy what's left of the season.

How, then, can we enjoy Christmas?

First, we must start early. That feeling we have when we see the first Christmas display (too early for most of us) must be turned into a petition: "O Lord, speak to me." We cannot wait until the break between rehearsing Act I and Act II to get into the Christmas spirit.

Second, we must daily commit ourselves.

Several years ago, Hugh Haynie, cartoonist for the Louisville *Courier-Journal,* featured a cartoon for Christmas Day that became tradition for many readers. As a man sat among stacks of gifts, reviewing his list one final time, he asked, "Let's see, have I forgotten anyone?" There in the background stood Jesus.

While many ministers used the cartoon as a reference in their Christmas sermons, assuming that the cartoon was obviously directed toward non-Christians, I saw something different—Christians whose season was too cluttered to see Christ.

Third, we should invite the Lord to guide our Advent events. Play and cantata rehearsals always go more smoothly when begun with prayer, even if they start 10 minutes late. We need to ask how the drama or music relates to the mission of the local church. We need to ask how we can reach beyond our walls, our circles of friendship, to touch lives with the Christmas message.

While Isaiah's words foretelling the Messiah are familiar in Christmas verse and music, another passage should bring hope to the anxious: "They that wait upon the Lord shall renew their strength; they shall mount up with wings as eagles; they shall run, and not be weary; and they shall walk, and not faint" (Isa. 40:31, KJV).

Christmas—
Single-Parent Style

O H, THERE'S NO PLACE like home for the holidays . . ." is a song of the season that reminds us that Christmas is a family time. Carols, television specials, and church programs often rest on the assumption that every family is composed of two active parents. Increasingly, however, there are "other" families—families that do not fit the traditional definition. Many teens in such families feel left out during Christmas.

Robert, age 14, has two Christmases—one with his mother on Christmas Eve and another with his father on Christmas Day. He's used to commuting between parents since their divorce five years ago.

Kelly, age 17, faces her first Christmas in a single-parent family. Her father deserted them and ran off with his secretary. They haven't received any support—financial or emotional—from him. Kelly realizes that this Christmas will be very different from previous ones.

Megan, age 15, prays daily for a reconciliation between her parents, hoping that memories of previous Christmases will draw her parents back together.

Elizabeth, age 13, doesn't have a father to remember. Her mother never married the man who got her pregnant. Elizabeth longs for a traditional Christmas.

Barry and Rod, 14 and 16, will be spending a Christmas without a mother who died this year; hopefully, their aunt will help their father make it a good Christmas "under the circumstances."

Single-parent families are created by divorce, death,

or pregnancy without marriage. The consequences, whatever the origin, can be devastating on the emotional and spiritual development of teens. In many ways, teens in single-parent homes created by death may have a slight economic advantage: The house may have been paid for through mortgage insurance, their parent is a recipient of pension and life insurance, and they are covered by Social Security. So Christmas deprivation may be more emotional than economic.

However, thousands of teens facing their first Christmas with one parent are learning that the stockings will be unstuffed. Some may skip lunch to save money for presents; others will try to find part-time jobs to raise enough cash for gifts.

Some teens react in anger. "Why did he have to do it to us?" one teen demanded after his father moved out. Many teens look at divorce as a personal rejection.

Although there has been a formal divorce, the hostilities between ex-mates may continue. Teens get wounded in the cross fire or can be used to get back at the other mate. Some parents use the Christmas season to "one-up" the other parent. One father groaned on Christmas night when his teens returned from their mother's apartment, loaded down with presents. "Hey, Dad, check this out! Look what Mom gave us!"

Some parents use presents to "make it up" to the teen for "All you've been through." They give expensive presents they cannot afford. Sadly, some teens—angry, hurt, confused—demand and expect expensive presents from their parents. Or they react like Ricky, angry at his father, refusing to buy a present for him or accept a gift from him. Some do not want to spend time with the other parent, or if forced to do so, can make the occasion most miserable for all.

"My father acts as if nothing has changed," scoffs

Nancy. "All year long he never comes around, then suddenly at Christmas, it's 'good ol' Dad.'"

"And what do you want good ol' Dad to bring you?"

"Things . . . the way it used to be," Nancy answered.

It's easy for teens like Nancy to envy the "familiness" of dual-parent families. When teens ask, "Why can't things be like they were?" or "Why can't we be like other families?" there are few answers that satisfy. Some families do manage, for the benefit of the children, to declare a truce and share Christmas Eve. But the first of the year reminds them that the problems still exist.

Some older teens are shouldered with adult financial and emotional responsibilities. As younger brothers' and sisters' eyes sparkle with all the potential gifts in the toy store, they are burdened with providing the basics. Many teens will go without so that younger brothers and sisters can have something.

With the remarriage rate so high, many teens will find themselves in a "blended" family this Christmas. Not all will be as tranquil as the "Brady Bunch," and not all teens will be as loved as Nicholas in "Eight Is Enough." The "step" world—stepparents, stepsiblings, stepgrandparents—creates a whole new protocol of Christmas traditions that have to be blended or abandoned.

So what can we do?

1. Teens from traditional families should be sensitive to those from single-parent homes. Some may be under heavy emotional and financial strain, unable to donate to every "pass the hat" for so-and-so's Christmas present.

2. Teens can help out in a single-parent family by contributing gratis baby-sitting. Most single parents really have to make their December dollars stretch. Single parents with young children have to hire a baby-sitter

with money that could be used for presents. So why not volunteer as a way of giving: "Congratulations! In the spirit of the season this coupon entitles you to four hours of free baby-sitting."

3. Many single-parent families, indeed a considerable percentage, are headed by women and fall below the poverty line. Why not adopt a one-parent family as a special project? Or teens might do Christmas baking and share the goodies.

4. Everyone can lend a listening ear during the Christmas season. Teens residing with one parent will be forced to make some rough decisions—no "Mom and Dad" gifts this year. Whom do they spend more on: Mom? or Dad? Some teens will want to unload their hurts. A few will be tempted to postpone Christmas. That would be unfortunate. Listen with a concerned heart and encourage them to make healthy decisions. Help them resist throwing a pity party. You can make a difference.

Teens need to be reminded that Jesus probably spent some of His life in a one-parent home. After the birth narratives and the visit to the Temple when Jesus was 12, we hear no more about Joseph. Because of the strength of the father in Jewish culture (even though we know Joseph was not the real father), this is a significant omission. Simply, the single-parent family is not new. The first one found in the Bible is in Genesis 21: The single mother was Hagar, her son Ishmael. Though banished to the desert area, the mother and son survived, and his descendants today, in Muslim nations, number in the millions.

This year, there are 12.5 million children and teens growing up in one-parent homes. For some of them, the greatest gift you could share is an introduction to Jesus Christ.

A Tree for Benji

JOHN STEVENS RUBBED HIS EYES as he stretched on the old couch in the living room. Today was December 21. Christmas was only four days away. Time was running out. How many times had eight-year-old Benji impatiently demanded, "When are we going to put up the tree?"

How could he tell him there wasn't going to be a tree this year? Last year—and the years before that—there had been a marriage, a reason to celebrate. Now . . . nothing. But that wasn't the real reason. There was that strange attitude of his dad, Benji's grandfather.

Eight months ago John had given up and moved in with his parents. Somehow, trying to pay the bills, care for the three boys, be father and mother, and deal with the gnawing hurt from the divorce demanded too much energy.

The old farmhouse, too, was overcrowded. His boys shared the tiny bedroom he had once shared with his three brothers, and now, more than he had as a child, John longed for a bedroom rather than the old living room couch.

Well, at least they were together. His mind went to Benji—the youngest child, the only one who kept talking about Jesus, and how He could do the impossible. He must have gotten that from some Sunday School. It certainly didn't run in the family. And how was Benji really dealing with the divorce? How many times had he asked about that tree?

John heard his father's telltale footsteps in the kitchen. The morning routine had not changed in decades. By the time John rolled out from under the covers, the coffee would be ready. Perhaps this was the morning to confront the old man about the tree.

He swung off the couch and shuffled into the kitchen.

"Morning," he said. His dad turned from the stove as though surprised to see him.

"Morning! Want some coffee?"

"Yeah, I better." John stretched again as he sat down to the same scarred table at which he had eaten almost every meal in his childhood. His dad placed a cup of steaming coffee in front of him, then slid the sugar and cream across the table.

"What's up today?" John asked.

"Thought I'd mend that fence." John noticed that his father assumed he knew which section. John pressed on.

"Soon be Christmas." The old man did not respond. John quickly took another sip of coffee, seeking courage.

"Benji keeps asking when we're going to put up a tree. I don't know what to tell him."

A long silence followed. The old man drained the last of his coffee and stared at the bottom of his mug.

"Dad?" John pleaded.

"Ever been a tree that you can remember?" the old man said, jerking his gaze from the mug to his son.

"No, Dad. And that's just it." Abruptly, the elder Stevens stood and moved without effort to the sink. He placed the mug on the drainboard and left the room.

John could not remember a Christmas tree in this house. For that reason, on the first Christmas of his marriage, he had squeezed the biggest tree he could find into their tiny apartment, mostly to spite the old man. His father had not even commented on it.

Why was his dad so against a Christmas tree? John

knew some people had religious objections, but his dad wasn't fond of churches.

He had not heard his mother's footsteps.

"Morning, Son," she mumbled. "Radio says it's 14 degrees outside. When you leave for work, be sure to bundle up." She reached for her coffee mug and poured the coffee. Then she joined her son at the table. "How did you sleep?"

"Fine." John didn't want to add another worry to his mom's overload.

"I'm concerned about your back, Son." John cut into the conversation, recycled from other mornings.

"Well, I've got more things than my back to worry 'bout." John stepped to the stove to pour another cup.

"Like Benji?" his mom asked.

"What about Benji? Has he been giving you problems?"

"That little guy's never a problem. But he sure is wanting a tree. That's all he talked about yesterday after he got home from school. A tree!"

"Well, I don't want him pestering you."

His mother cut him off. "Grandmothers delight in being pestered. He tells me most things on his mind. Eight-year-olds can't store much in their silos." She gestured toward her head. John moved his chair closer to his mother's.

"Mom, why hasn't there been a Christmas tree in this house?"

Before she spoke, his mother stroked a rough place on the tabletop. Then she said, "You asked me Benji's question every Christmas until you were 10." Her voice conveyed no trace of annoyance. "Funny . . . Benji is so much like you . . . takes me back. He is the spitting image of you." John could not be certain if his mother was merely stalling or was completely avoiding the question.

"Mom, why isn't there a tree?" John tried to keep the desperation from his voice.

"Same answer now as then. Just, 'cause."

"That's no answer for Benji. He's smart."

John's mother looked away, her eyes brimming. "Then I don't know! I never remember a tree, and I've lived in this house for 40 years. Your dad don't like questions when he makes up his mind on something!"

"Did you ever ask him?"

"Once."

"What did he say?"

"Nothing. He just sat there in that rocking chair of his and stared at the wall."

John would have pressed the subject, but chimes from the old clock on the fireplace mantel drifted to the kitchen, reminding him he was late. The questions would have to wait.

Ten hours later, John pulled off the paved road and onto the gravel road that led to the farmhouse. He was exhausted from another day at the plant. Abruptly, Benji and his old mangy dog darted into his path. John stopped the car and rolled down the window.

"Been waiting for you," Benji said. "Wanna show you something." John took his foot off the brake, and the car started. "No, Dad. I want to show you something!" Benji pleaded.

"What?" John snapped.

"Come on." Benji turned and bolted toward the woods. His dog barked once and followed. John turned the motor off and climbed out of the car. A blast of cold wind stung him. Whatever Benji wanted him to see must be important to risk this wind. Fortunately, Benji didn't run far.

"There it is." John couldn't follow his gesture.

"What, Benji?" he demanded impatiently.

"That's the one . . . that's the tree I want Granddad to put up for Christmas." The impact of the words were as raw as the December wind. "It's just right!" Benji proudly stated. John looked at a tree that would cost about $75.00 in the city.

"We'll have to think about it." The sentence escaped John before he considered its impact. He angrily kicked a frozen clod of dirt. Why not tell Benji the truth. There wasn't going to be a tree. He turned and walked rapidly toward the car.

"Dad?" Benji protested.

"Come on. Grandma's got supper waiting."

The little fellow turned for one last look at the tree. "See you tomorrow," he said and bolted toward the car.

They drove to the house in silence. If only Benji knew how many trees John had picked out before he quit trying to change his Dad's mind.

John looked at this son huddled against the passenger door.

"What's wrong, pardner?"

"Nothing." But John recognized the hurt. Benji opened the door and ran toward the house.

John slammed his hand against the steering wheel, more from frustration than anger. Now he'd have to confront his dad in a way no son should.

The house was silent; the boys asleep. The three adults had silently watched TV. As the theme song of the late news announced the hour, John's father stood and remarked, "Getting late," his equivalent of "Good night."

"Dad, I need to talk to you." The old man switched off the TV. "Dad, Benji is wanting a Christmas tree. He's been through so much. And, well, I know this is your house and we're guests here, but how do I tell an eight-year-old, 'No tree'?"

There was a long silence. John couldn't be sure his mother was still in the room.

"Tell him there's never been a tree," the old man retorted, too sharply for John's comfort. But still John thought he sensed a softening. He pressed on.

"He'll want to know why."

Another silence—this one longer. Then his father spoke slowly. "I was Benji's age. We'd gone down to the Perkins' place and cut the tree I'd picked out. It was a beauty. Back then we owned all that land. Pulled that tree home and put it up right there in that corner." He pointed toward the stairwell.

"We didn't have ornaments like most folk. Just popcorn strings and some ribbons. But it was pretty enough. My mama helped us string that popcorn and told us Christmas stories." The old man stopped. Only the ticking of the mantel clock broke the silence.

"Mama . . ." The old man stopped again and cleared his throat. "Mama died that next day. Hadn't even been sick. She was the one who had trusted Jesus, and she was the one who died. I couldn't understand it all."

John edged forward on the couch because his father's words were whispered. "We didn't have funeral homes around here then. People were laid out at home. So we had to take down the tree to put her casket there."

Suddenly, John's heart strained with his dad. How could an eight-year-old deal with that ugly invasion? He saw his mother's tear-filled eyes dart from him to her husband.

"My mama was buried on Christmas Day . . . and I've never felt like celebrating."

After a moment John spoke, carefully struggling for words. "Dad, why didn't you tell me before now?"

"Every Christmas comes, I think about it. Can't

seem to get it out of my mind," he said in his usual evasive way. Then the clock struck the half hour. As if on signal, the old man looked at the clock, then resumed his stoic posture. "Getting late," he said as he shuffled out of the room.

If John expected a comment from his mother, he was disappointed. "Turn out the lights, John, when you go to bed." But her words were spoken softly.

Later, in the darkened room, John sat listening to the systematic ticktock of the mantel clock. He turned to confront it. The clock had been a gift for his grandparents on their wedding day. How many other memories of that woman remained in this farmhouse to tease the 8-year-old child that cowered within the toughness of the 69-year-old farmer-father?

Finally, he punched the pillows in his nightly ritual. Tomorrow was December 23. Somehow he'd have to find a way to explain to Benji. Although he didn't know much about the Bible, perhaps he could tie it into the Christmas story. Wasn't there something about a tree symbolizing eternal life? And Benji's great-grandmother had evidently been a believer. John turned restlessly, trying to fit the pieces together.

A few feet away, behind the security of the white bedroom door, tears trickled down the old man's face and wet the pillowcase. Sally Stevens had slept with this man for 50 years and had never seen a mood like this one. She called his name, but there was no response.

The next afternoon, as Benji raced down the front steps of Martin Elementary School, he was greeted by a different horn. He discovered his granddad's old, exhausted '53 truck.

"Hi, Granddad," he said as he got in and pulled the rickety old door shut. The old man started the tired engine and pulled away from the curb.

"Have a good day, boy?" the old man asked. Benji recited what a great time they had had this last day of school before the Christmas break. The truck sputtered along old, bumpy roads heading home. When they turned down the lane leading to the woods, no explanation was offered or requested.

"See all that land over there, boy?" the old man asked. "My daddy, your great-granddaddy, used to own all this. When I was your age I'd come down here and fight Indians." His voice gave the threat of danger.

"Real Indians?" Benji asked, his eyes the size of half-dollars.

The old man laughed. "No, boy. Pretend Indians. This was my favorite place in the whole world." He pulled off the road and hopped out of the truck.

"Boy, you see that tree?" He raised his arm to identify a tall tree in a clump.

Benji whispered, "Yes, sir."

"When I was your age, I wanted to chop down that tree and take it home."

"Really, granddad? Wasn't it awfully big to take home?"

"Ah, boy," he said with a laugh. "It wasn't that big then . . . it was like, well, that one over there." Benji's eyes followed the old man's gesture to the very tree he had picked out the other day.

"Granddad," he exclaimed, "that would sure make a pretty Christmas tree." After a moment he added, "Wouldn't it?"

From deep within the old man's spirit, the voice that responded was not one tarnished by years of denial, but an eight-year-old boy's.

"Sure would, boy. Sure would! Go get the ax . . . in the truck."

The old man swung the ax with the skill of years. One more solid swing of the ax would topple the cedar tree. The old man stopped. "Put out your hands, boy." Benji complied. "Here, you bring her down." Benji started to question. "You can do it—your own Christmas tree."

Benji's eyes widened. His mind spun. Imagine, cutting his own Christmas tree . . . no one else in his old school could do that.

Benji swung the ax. The tree swayed, slid slowly to the ground. Benji squealed with glee.

"Good job, boy. Good job!"

John knew what he would say—or at least what he thought he would tell Benji. For 10 miles he had carefully rehearsed his lines. Hopefully, he had anticipated every question Benji would ask.

He got out of his car and walked toward the porch. Taking a deep breath, he opened the screen door and turned the old porcelain knob. His first thoughts were that he was in the wrong house. There stood a huge cedar tree filling the corner where he imagined one other tree once had stood.

John looked to the old man for a word of explanation.

"Boy picked out a good one, didn't he?"

In that moment, father and son spoke a new language. Benji stared at them only a moment. Then he returned to hanging the ornaments his grandmother handed him.

"It's a tree for Benji," the old man said brightly, although his chin wobbled. "For Benji."

Then the final tears of a long season fell from the eyes of a 69-year-old man who, as a boy, also had been called Benji.

A Poet's Gift

Tears

The tears stung;
    They must have.
The young girl,
    innocent of all the accusations
    and idle talk.

"Why me?"
Ah, to be with child
    and yet
"Unknown?" by any man,
    let alone
    a carpenter.

Perhaps she should not
    have run away
    from the neighbor's
    menacing questions.
After all, everyone knew
    the power of that woman's tongue.

Somehow,
    it seemed different,
    now that Mary
    was the subject
    of the gossip.

How Can It Be?

He struck harder.
With greater force than ever before summoned,
He brought down the hammer
    again and again.
The nail long before had reached its
    union with the wood.
His mind was not on his work
    but the hurt within his spirit.

With child . . . down came the hammer!
With CHILD . . . down came the hammer!
Not his . . . down came the hammer!
Not his . . . down came the hammer!
WHOSE?

"Joseph," an alarmed voice demanded,
    "What's wrong, man?"
Joseph snapped to reality,
    embarrassed by the call of another craftsman.
"You've been flailing with that hammer
    like you're building a ship's rudder
    rather than a table."
Joseph looked down at the telltale marks
    where hammer had assaulted
    new soft wood.
A sloppy craftsman's signature,
    not that of Joseph's.

His great shoulders wept with strain.
    They wanted to release the hurt
    captured in his spirit.

His world: a carpenter's shop
            a small village, Nazareth,
            a woman, Mary,
Now lay amiss.
She's with child—the words hammered
      now on the anvil of his spirit.
With child!
But whose child?

The hammer fell from his hand
      with a thud
      to the hard dirt floor.
Joseph turned, and without words
      strode out of his shop,
      his mind far, far from carpentry.

The Visitors

"Joseph . . . Joseph! Wake up!"

Joseph rolled onto his side, away from her.
"Joseph . . . I hear voices!"
But the carpenter would not stir
      from his night sleep
      until she shook him.
Lying in the silent, measured breathing
      of the animals,
      he, too, heard the voices.

He rolled to his side and crept away from
    the mother and Child.
At the entrance he saw
    flickering lamps
    held by several people.
Ah, more poor tourists seeking
    inexpensive lodging.
"Who is it?" Mary called in the darkness.

Now they were talking, and
    Mary wished she could hear
    what they were saying.
Joseph could talk with anyone
    about anything,
    even in the middle of the night.

"Mary, they want to see the Baby."
    "What?"
"They want to see the Child."
    "Who does?"
"Shepherds . . . they've come to see the Baby."
Joseph looked at his wife—she looked tired.
    It seemed so unfair to ask her
    to let the men invade their privacy,
    but they were so insistent.
Besides, Mary would feel uncomfortable
    with these strange men.
After all, she'd been gawked at
    all along the journey,
    and how many old wives' tales
    and scoldings had they listened to
    during the trip here,
    and now so soon after birth.

Finally, he picked up the small crib
     and carried it out to where
     the shepherds stood.
In that moment—that brief moment—
     he had clearly heard
     the most beautiful music—
     there, from within the stable;
     yet that seemed impossible.
But he never forgot the shepherds.
Never had he seen men more excited
     over a child.
They danced.
They clapped.
They laughed.
And right in the midst of their celebration
     the Child awoke
     and lay, awake.
They rejoiced over the Child.
Jews did for any male child,
     but this celebration
     seemed special.

Joseph basked in the moment,
     aware that this male Child, not his,
     was that special.

Interlude

The Child slept silently against the mother's breast,
    and Joseph decided they could do
    without him for a while.
After all these days in stable poor
    with taxes honored,
    there was little left.

So, it was time to go to work,
    to put the experience in perspective.
Now there would be three mouths to feed,
    all the more reason to work.
And the way the Child nursed,
    He would not grow to be a weakling.

So, he nodded to the mother
    and slipped away.
At the stable entrance he turned
    to notice
    the warming sight:
    mother and Child, asleep.

Something of that scene
    touched his spirit
    with a soothing breath of peace
    he had never known before.

Whatever lay ahead, he reasoned,
    they were family.

The Evening

Finally,
 the wretched wailing
 and staccatoed screaming
 had ended.
Now the women wept,
 silent tears
 that slowly emptied
 reservoirs of tears.
Moaning prevailed.

The innkeeper's stock of wine
 was depleted
 before the memories
 could be calmed.

The soldiers' weaponry
 Shined again,
 but only after an afternoon's
 cleaning
 had produced
 a mountain of soiled linen—
 stained by infants' blood.

Mothers held the lifeless forms
 near their breasts
 while the silent tears
 streamed down their faces.
And in their hearts
 revenge screamed for attention.

And they asked for Mary.
"Gone."
"GONE?"
"Gone!"

The Father's Touch

How he laughed, all teeth shining,
    as he watched the Boy
    struggling with the saw.
"Let your shoulders do the work!"
    And the young Boy turned,
    forehead dripping with sweat,
    the chin never more determined,
    and again launched His attack.

Already the father was pleased
    with the Boy's knowledge of woods
    and the manly handling of the tools.
This lad was unlike many boys His age
    who were slow;
Jesus seemed to learn quickly.

Joseph watched until he knew his help was needed.
So he went and stood just behind Jesus.
Leaning over, his hands behind the Boy's,
    together they worked for a while.
Then he withdrew
    to let the Boy continue
    until the plank dropped in two—
And the Boy turned, with an enormous grin,
    and accepted Joseph's pat on the shoulder.
"Good job . . . good job!"

Christmas Frenzy

Between Christmas play rehearsals
    and part-time jobs,
    the Sunday School class party
    and the choir rehearsal . . .

Between baby-sitting for a little extra money
    and a term paper due before Christmas break
    and mad dashes here and there,
    trying to find just the right gift
    while stretching the budget to include
        gift-wrapping . . .

Comes the invitation:
    —not to give to one more group gift fund
    —not to throw one more party
    —not to contribute to one more charity

But —to make this Christmas special.

Christmas Reflection

One of our Christmas problems is
the blitz of items we could buy for
someone or wish someone would buy
for us. Luxury bombards our
senses till we're dulled.

Let's face it, there comes the morning
when the kid races through,
opening all his presents, and then looks up
in complete innocence and asks,
"Is this all there is?"

Rather, Christmas is discovered by a
small child who uses his resources—
however limited—to purchase a gift
for that "someone" in his life.

Whether wrapped in an array or disarray,
there is a nourished hope
that anticipates the unwrapping.

And in that moment of opening,
the child understands Christmas.
But somewhere en route, in growing up,
we lose that innocence.

Christmas is risk,
    a reaching out
    with neither dollar signs nor
    equal signs explain.

Christmas always costs something—
    but it costs more
    not to celebrate.

Repeat
the Sounding Joy

It's impossible to sing "Joy to the World"
like it is supposed to be sung.
I'm not in the joyful mood this Christmas.
I tried to sing it this morning,
but I couldn't see the words
because of the tears
and that sizable lump in my throat
and the ache in my spirit.
I simply couldn't sing with the congregation.
You know last New Year's Eve
we talked about
what this year would bring.
But I had no idea this December
would bring a solo Christmas.
But even though my voice
was not heard beyond my pew,
I heard the words
echoing in my soul:
"Repeat the sounding joy . . ."
and I did.
I loved you,
I loved,
I was loved,
I will be loved again.
"Repeat the sounding joy!"
I was loved,
I will be loved again.
"Repeat the sounding joy!"

Simplicity

Most of us keep hoping for that
ten-carat Christmas—
the really special one
whose memory never fades.

But amid the grandiose
plans and schemes and plots,
We fail to note the simplicity
of the first Christmas—
the birth of the Child.

I Believe

I BELIEVE
in a Christmas that cannot
be limited to 24 hours
on the 25th of December.

I BELIEVE
in a Christmas, future,
when all God's children
will be home.

I BELIEVE
that in our first moment in heaven
we will realize
how much He gave

to spend those years among us
to invite us
to spend forever with Him.

I BELIEVE
that His coming
locked the world
into a loving embrace.

We've Come to Another Christmas Season

My, how time flies. And still the
need in so many lives for
a special Christmas:

One that warms the heart,
not just when a gift is opened,
or at the church Christmas play,
or the first time the tree is lit.

There is an Advent of the heart,
in the quiet corridors of your
spirit:
Where no decorations clutter,
Where no fakey Santa looks bored or weary,
Where no carolers stroll—
There Advent is celebrated.

My wish for you
    is a moment,
    least expected,
    unplanned,
    perhaps at the moment
    you need it most,
Someone will say:
    "MERRY CHRISTMAS!"

And all the power of those two
    words will resound within your
    spirit.

The Writers' Gifts

A Catalog of Christmas Quotes

IF WE COULD IMAGINE crowding the Pacific Ocean into a teakettle, we can get a glimpse of the miracle of trying to crowd God into human form.

—*D. Shelby Corlett*

———————

THE LORD OF GLORY stooped to be the Babe of the Manger that no proud group of men might ever say, He is ours exclusively.

—*G. B. Williamson*

———————

A CHRISTLESS CHRISTMAS, if such were possible, would be like counterfeit money. It might have the appearance, but no value.

—*W. T. Purkiser*

———————

WHEN I THINK OF THE CHRISTMAS STORY it makes me so happy. Do you know why? Because I know that the Baby Jesus was born in Bethlehem for the whole world—also for you and me. You and I know much more than the shepherds—or even the wise men— knew. We know that Jesus died on the Cross for the sins of the whole world—also for your sins and mine . . . I believe it. I don't understand it, but that does not matter.

—*Corrie ten Boom*

He was a world-maker before he was a carpenter.

—*Phineas F. Bresee*

Christmas is not just a date on our calendar; it is a state of the heart.

—*Dale Evans Rogers*

Millions have been lifted out of the sleep of unhappy, purposeless lives into abundant life by the gift of faith in this Christ. . . . On whatever day they accepted this gift from Him, that day is Christmas to them forever.

—*Dale Evans Rogers*

How could this cow-stall Child be a Savior, Christ, the Lord? Were the problems of those shepherds so small that they needed no more savior than that? The promises of the coming Messiah, some of them now very old, spoke of the grandeur, the power, the might, and the glory of that great One. There was no word of cow barns at the rear doors of inns in tiny, insignificant towns.

—*Paul Bassett*

For you know: If our Lord were born a thousand times in Bethlehem and not in you, you would be lost anyhow. Oh, for your life's sake, accept His offer—do not send Him away with the answer: No place for You!

—*Casper ten Boom*

I'VE LEARNED THAT IF I CAN just get into the spirit of that original Christmas Gift, I won't have any problem increasing my joy and happiness this Christmas or in Christmases to come!

—*J. B. Chapman*

CHRIST, THE INCARNATION, the birth of Jesus Christ is the triumph of love over hate. It is the stubborn refusal of divine holiness to be altered or defeated by human sin.

—*W. E. McCumber*

CHRISTMAS IS THE ONLY LIGHT in the tunnel of history.

—*W. E. McCumber*

GOD'S CHOICE OF TINY BETHLEHEM was not a fluke. It was not a 54th choice. He meant to have the Christ child born there—and so He means to enter wherever He knocks.

—*Paul Bassett*

THE WORLD IS LARGE AND COMPLEX, and sometimes there seems to be no sacred ground. But in tent and palace, in adobe hut and castle, in barrack prison and under lighted trees across the lands, the language of Christmas is universal.

—*Marcus Bach*

CHRISTMAS IS A TIME FOR "GIVING OUT," real giving, not swapping!

—*Anonymous*

HOW MANY OBSERVE CHRIST'S BIRTHDAY; how few His precepts! O! 'tis easier to keep holidays than commandments.

—*Benjamin Franklin*

MARY AND JOSEPH WERE BUSY being competent Jewish parents, doting over their Firstborn, passing Him back and forth, feeding Him and changing Him—knowing how very dependent He was upon them. The whole thing was amazing! He was dependent upon them. Could this helpless Newcomer be the very Son of God who led Israel across the Red Sea dry-shod? Could this bawling Babe be the Offspring of Yahweh? ... Could this frail Youngster be the very inspiration of the prophets—Isaiah, Micah, and the rest?

—*Paul Bassett*

EVERY LITTLE CHILD IN ALL THE WORLD has been a little safer since the coming of the Christ of Bethlehem.

—*Roy L. Smith*

THE HINGE OF HISTORY is on the door of a Bethlehem stable.

—*Ralph W. Sockman*

CHRISTMAS BEGAN IN THE HEART OF GOD. It is complete only when it reaches the heart of man.

—*Religious Telescope*

I WISH WE COULD put some of the Christmas spirit in jars and open a jar of it every month.

—*Harlan Miller*

IT IS GOOD TO BE CHILDREN sometimes, and never better than at Christmas, when its mighty Founder was a child himself.

—*Charles Dickens*

Formed in a virgin womb, God's only begotten Son shared her life by way of a fragile umbilical cord. The divine Savior entered the limits of frail human care. Though His conception was supernatural, the Christ faced the risks of childbirth. His infant body was nourished through Mary's bloodstream, and then at her breast. This Baby Jesus lay vulnerable in the loving arms of a first-time mother, chosen from David's royal line of faith.

—Ivan Beals

The virgin birth was sheer miracle, the marvelous work of God. It is the method God chose to introduce His Eternal Son into human history. You and I come *out* of history. He came *into* history.

Jesus as the Son of God came into history from outside, so He must come into me from outside. By the same Spirit of God who formed Him in the womb of the Virgin Mary, Christ must be formed in me.

—W. M. Greathouse

I love to look at that star: it doesn't seem as if Christmas would be quite the same if there had been no beautiful glowing star, sparkling like a jewel in the clear, cold heavens.

—J. B. Chapman

THIS CHRISTMAS I LOOK INTO THE EYES of another Child—the Child whose gift of himself cost something tremendous. The price is unmatched in the history of the world. It is beyond human comprehension that God could care so much that He would show His love in such a tangible way.

—Mary E. Latham

I MUST ALLOW MY OWN PERSONAL LIFE to become a "Bethlehem" for the Son of God. Within my own being, by the Holy Spirit, there must be a miraculous birth of Christ.

—W. M. Greathouse

JESUS CHRIST . . . the perpetual Christmas Gift to all ages!

—D. Shelby Corlett

MANY WILL BE MEASURING the impact of December 25 by the gross national product, the balance of payments, or the volume of merchandise moved. The brutal reality is that these material indicators have a way of affecting us all. By contrast, we should be remembering a baby and the significance of His birth in our world.

—Jerald D. Johnson

NOTHING HAS HAPPENED in the march—or muddle—of history more significant for human welfare than Christmas.

—*W. E. McCumber*

_____

EVER SINCE THE DAYS of the first Christmas, the world has been divided into two groups: those who were ready for Christmas; those who were not ready.

—*G. Weatherley*

_____

AT BETHLEHEM WE DISCOVER JESUS beginning His journey to Calvary to redeem lost men.

—*Orville W. Jenkins*

_____

NEITHER SANTA CLAUS, nor Rudolph, nor the number of shopping days till Christmas can destroy what took place in Bethlehem. Nothing can wipe out history, nor can anything impede our access to the manger to present our gifts there!

—*Morris Chalfant*

TRUTH HAS NO SPECIAL TIME of its own. Its hour is now—always.

—Albert Schweitzer

HE WOULD ADORE MY GIFTS instead of Me, and rest in nature, not the God of nature: So both should losers be.

—George Herbert

GOOD WORDS are worth much and cost less.

—George Herbert

I AM IN THE HABIT of looking not so much to the nature of a gift as to the spirit in which it is offered.

—Robert Louis Stevenson

EVERY GOOD GIFT and every perfect gift is from above, and cometh down from the Father of lights, with whom is no variableness, neither shadow of turning.

—James 1:17, KJV

PRECIOUS ARE ALL THINGS that come from friends.
—*Theocritus*

IF JESUS CHRIST were to come today, people would not crucify Him. They would ask Him to dinner and hear what He had to say, and make fun of Him.
—*Thomas Carlyle*

WE TEND, SOMETIMES, to emphasize this part of Christmas to the point of seeming to exclude the intellectual. I am glad that poor, uneducated shepherds saw the star and heard the angel's song. The vision and the message transformed their lives, giving them new hope. But I am also glad that a revelation came by the light of that same star to wise men who were no less obedient to the heavenly vision.
—*Ruth A. Cameron*

CHRISTMAS IS A WONDERFUL SEASON of the year—the beautiful wintry scenes; the preparation for homecoming gatherings and holiday meals and entertainment; the purchasing, wrapping, and secretive storing of gifts; the look of wonder and anticipation in the faces of little children around the Christmas tree; the logs burning in the fireplace casting out their warmth and cheery glow; the great church music that lifts the soul of every worshiper; the church's children's Christmas program, which always brings its laughter and tears, its joys and surprises. These and hundreds of other things mean Christmas to Christians around the world.

—*Orville W. Jenkins*

GOD IS NOT SANTA CLAUS. He does not bestow upon an excited and greedy world that which costs Him nothing. He does not make an easy magical pilgrimage across rooftops to spend a seasonal happiness. God gives at the cost of self-sacrifice. At the cost of a manger and a cross and a grave, at the cost of rejected and slandered love. He gives continually because He loves eternally.

—*W. E. McCumber*

CHRISTMAS WILL BE FULL OF WONDER indeed, if, because of a spiritual celebration, there will be an accompanying spiritual commitment.

—*Jerald D. Johnson*

JESUS WASN'T BORN AT MACY'S but in a manger!

—*W. E. McCumber*

———————————

LITTLE JACK HORNER sat in the corner,
　　Eating a Christmas pie.
He put in his thumb and pulled out a plum,
　　And said, "What a good boy am I!"

—*Anonymous*

———————————

CHRISTMAS WON'T BE CHRISTMAS without any presents.

—*Louisa May Alcott, "Little Women"*

———————————

BACKWARD, TURN BACKWARD, O Time, in your flight,
Make me a child again just for tonight!

—*Elizabeth Akers Allen*

———————————

CHRISTMAS IS A-COMING, the geese are getting fat;
Please to put a penny in the old man's hat;
If you haven't got a penny, a ha' penny will do,
If you haven't got a ha' penny, God bless you!

—*Anonymous*

Liberality consists less in giving a great deal than in gifts well-timed.

—*Jean de la Bruyere*

Whatever it is, I fear Greeks even when they bring gifts.

—*Virgil*

Who could know heaven save by heaven's Gift?

—*Marcus Manilius*

Never look a gift horse in the mouth.

—*Jerome*

At Christmas play and make good cheer,
For Christmas comes but once a year.

—*Thomas Tusser*

A Christmas gambol oft could cheer
The poor man's heart through half the year.

—*Sir Walter Scott*

I WEAR THE CHAIN I forged in life (says Marley's ghost).

—*Charles Dickens*

———————

I'M DREAMING of a white Christmas.

—*Irving Berlin*

———————

FATHER CALLS ME WILLIAM, Sister calls me Will,
Mother calls me Willie, but the fellers call me Bill!

Most all the time, the whole year round,
     There ain't no flies on me,
But jest 'fore Christmas
     I'm as good as I kin be!

—*Eugene Field*

———————

IT SEEMED SO STRANGE on such slender thread as the feeble throb of an infant life the salvation of the world should hang and no special watch care over its safety, no better shelter be provided it than a "stable," no other cradle than a manger! And it is still true.

—*Alfred Edersheim*

Jesus was born twice. The birth at Bethlehem was a birth into a life of weakness. The second time He was born from the grave—"the firstborn from the dead"—into the glory of heaven and the throne of God.

—*Andrew Murray*

The shepherds did not go to Bethlehem seeking the birth of a great man, or a famous teacher, or national hero. They were promised a Savior.

—*Handel H. Brown*

The whole question of the virgin birth of Jesus need not afflict the average man. If Jesus is unique, unlike any other person, it is not illogical to believe that His birth was unique.

—*William Lyon Phelps*

It is possible to give without loving, but it is impossible to love without giving.

—*Richard Braunstein*

God's gifts put man's best dreams to shame.

—*Elizabeth Barrett Browning*

THE MANNER OF GIVING is worth more than the gift.

—*Pierre Corneille*

WE MAKE A LIVING by what we get, but we make a life by what we give.

—*Sir Winston Churchill*

GOD HAS GIVEN US two hands—one for receiving and the other for giving.

—*Billy Graham*

GIVING IS A JOY if we do it in the right spirit. It all depends on whether we think of it as "What can I spare?" or as "What can I share?"

—*Esther York Burkholder*

THE MAN WHO GIVES LITTLE with a smile gives more than the man who gives much with a frown.

—*Anonymous*

Gɪᴠᴇ ᴡɪᴛʜ ᴀ ᴡᴀʀᴍ ʜᴀɴᴅ, not a cold one.

—Anonymous

Gᴏᴅ ʙʟᴇss ᴜs every one!" said Tiny Tim, the last of all.

—Charles Dickens

Tʜᴇ Rᴇʟɪɢɪᴏᴜs ᴘᴇᴏᴘʟᴇ ᴏғ Cʜʀɪsᴛ's ᴅᴀʏ felt that the real messiah would only associate with holy men, and that His entry into the world would be triumphant, a victorious king who had come to reestablish His throne, literally. So, when Christ was born in a manger, among animals and refuse, and cold, they had a difficult time accepting Him. For Christ's expression of kingship begins, not in the palaces of men's hearts, but in their mangers.

—Andy Comiskey

Lᴇᴛ's ғᴀᴄᴇ ᴛʜᴇ ᴛʀᴜᴛʜ; as adults, Christmas rarely has the same intense excitement and thrill it held for us as children. The burdens of life that we have faced this year are not going to vanish behind some tinsel and holiday wreaths. A wayward son or daughter returning home for the holidays will generate some anxiety, so let's stop trying to compare old memories with the present. We can be thankful for happy memories of past holiday celebrations, but it doesn't help this Christmas to continually dwell on the past.

—*Anonymous*

Despite the insistent messages of the world, Christmas joy does not come from outward circumstances. It comes from within us. It does not depend on how many carols we sing, how many people we have around us, how many presents we receive.

—*Anonymous*

It was always said of him, that he knew how to keep Christmas well.

—*Charles Dickens*

The only gift is a portion of thyself.

—*Ralph Waldo Emerson*

THEIR DISCOVERY WAS TOO GREAT for them to contain in silence. They became the first evangels of the Lord Jesus and "made known abroad the saying which was told them concerning this child." Not only so, but when they returned to common tasks, they did so "glorifying and praising God for all the things that they had heard and seen." And as with every man who has found Christ, they discovered that those common tasks were graciously transfigured by reason of the fact that they had seen the Anointed One.

—J. Glenn Gould

———————

THIS IMPORTANT EVENT, which brought wise men from the East, shepherds from the hills, angels singing from heaven, a new star out of God's eternity, and the jealousy of wicked Herod, can never be forgotten. Its very importance has been its own preservation.

—Noble J. Hamilton

———————

HIS LIFE WAS THREATENED from the first. Knowing all this, He came because He loved us. God became like us that we might become like Him.

—D. Shelby Corlett

CHRISTMAS IS NOT ONLY A DAY in December; it is every time our tears are wiped away; every time new hope arises like a star in our dark night of the spirit; every time a sinner is saved by grace; every time a heart is filled with the Holy Spirit; every time a Blood-washed pilgrim enters into life eternal!

—*Earl G. Lee*

———————

THE CRIB AND THE CROSS were made of the same material, ordinary wood. But the Crown is of pure gold and sparkling jewels.

—*W. T. Purkiser*

———————

THE REAL CHRISTMAS MESSAGE is that God would save men, and to Him this saving was worth any cost it would require.

—*D. Shelby Corlett*

CHRISTMAS IS THE BIRTHDAY of a Friend, the best friend any of us ever had, or could have; a friend who has done more to prove His friendship than any other ever has, or could.

—*Clarence Edwin Flynn*

———————

HISTORY WAS REBORN when Christ came. Newspapers may fill their pages with attacks on everything Christ and His gospel stand for, yet in the date that appears at the top of each page all men unconsciously recognize the event which divides the centuries into B.C. and A.D.—the birth of Christ.

—*W. T. Purkiser*

———————

EVEN THE MAN ON THE STREET is beginning to look for the Christ. He sees very little hope of avoiding sociological and technological catastrophes without Him, as people continue to ruin the environment, waste their resources, manufacture their missiles, build their bombs, and mass-produce their gadgets, while they hurry frantically from pleasure to pleasure.

—*James McGraw*

WHAT MORE MEANINGFUL MESSAGE could be produced to a world given to fighting; driven mad by hate; bent on devastation, destruction, and death; and filled with suspicion and distrust—our world—than the old, old Christmas message that God loves and cares for the world.

—*D. Shelby Corlett*

I BELIEVE JESUS WOULD HAVE US make a divine Christmas list; why not ask for and receive the greatest Gift of all: the gift of the Holy Spirit?

—*Earl G. Lee*

TODAY IN THE HUMBLEST COTTAGE in the most obscure village some family is partaking of a meager meal and exchanging some small tokens of love, because He came into the world. And He has known similar circumstances.

—*Doris Schumann*

THE PALACE AND THE STABLE met in open combat. And the stable emerged victorious.

—*Hendrik van Loon*

THE "GLITTER BEFORE CHRISTMAS" turns to the "litter after Christmas."

—*W. T. Purkiser*

IF GOD BELIEVES in the possibility of redeeming a world of men, if He demonstrates His faith in the giving of His Son, surely we can have faith in man and in his possibility of redemption.

—*D. Shelby Corlett*

IF YOU HAVE NOT SENSED HIS PRESENCE, you are missing something exciting and wonderful, and maybe you are missing it because of some very simple circumstance that could be changed, just as the wise men changed their approach and quickly found Him—not in a palace, but in an ordinary house.

—*James McGraw*

IT IS NOT THAT WE SHOULD MAKE LESS of Christ's birth, but that we should make more of His life and His atoning death. If we stop at the manger in our thoughts of Christmas, we have not even read aright the Gospel record. It was only 40 days after the birth of the Savior that the Infant was brought for dedication to the Temple and Simeon said to Mary, "This child is destined to cause the falling and rising of many in Israel, and to be a sign that will be spoken against, so that the thoughts of many hearts will be revealed. And a sword will pierce your own soul too." The long shadow of the Cross fell even then across the scene.

—*W. T. Purkiser*

THE REAL PREPARATION FOR CHRISTMAS is the same this year as it has always been, "Let every heart prepare Him room."

—*George Coulter*

IF CHRISTIANS DON'T WITNESS of the redemptive, life-changing power of God at any other time of the year, they surely should at Christmas. What better time to tell the Good News than at a season when the whole world is aware of, if not truly celebrating, the birth of Christ, who provided for their salvation.

—*Aarlie J. Hull*

MAKE SURE YOU LOOK FOR HIM in the right places. While you are preoccupied with status, you may find Him in a stable.

—*James McGraw*

THE WORD RENDERED "HEAVENLY HOST" should properly be rendered army of heaven." It was not simply a choir of angelic voices, as we commonly view it. The choirs of praise and adoration assumed a magnitude far beyond our most fantastic imagining!

—*J. Glenn Gould*

OUR CHRISTMAS GIFTS come nearer to the original idea of Christmas when we love and give to those who cannot repay, to those who may not merit or in a sense fully appreciate them; when our gifts are sacrifices, gifts that cost us something, gifts that have saving or redeeming value in them.

—D. Shelby Corlett

SURELY ONLY THOSE without souls would despise carols!

—Noble J. Hamilton

THEY PROBABLY GAVE UP LOOKING directly at the star as they approached Jerusalem, and, thinking the new king would most certainly be born there, allowed their logic to interfere with God's leading.

—Nelson G. Mink

BECAUSE GOD ENTERED HUMAN HISTORY as a helpless child, the helpless have hope.

Because He reigns as King of Kings and Lord of Lords, we serve Him.

Because He first loved us, we love Him—and one another.

—Chuck Colson

THOSE WISE MEN OF OLD did not wait until everything was clearly revealed to them before following its gleam; they started and were led along the way, received unfolding revelations of it . . . It led them to Him who was born King of the Jews.

—J. Glenn Gould

OUR LORD MADE CHILDHOOD SACRED not only by the patience and tender interest He showed in children during His ministry, but by coming into the world as a little child and passing through the humble period of dependence and trust.

—Orval J. Nease

THEY GAVE HIM FRANKINCENSE as an evidence of their surrender and because their altars would no longer need the smoke of incense and perfume.

—Fred M. Weatherford

EVERYTHING INDICATES THAT THE WAY TO CHRIST is open to all. If He had been born in a private house, even though the house were ever so humble, the symbol would have indicated that His coming was private. But He was born at an inn—a house that welcomes everyone, in the stable of the inn—where the lowest can come. In the fullest possible way all the circumstances say, "Come to Christ—come just as you are!"

—J. B. Chapman

A GOOD CONSCIENCE is a continual Christmas!

—*Benjamin Franklin*

THERE NEVER WAS ANY HEART truly great and generous, that was not also tender and compassionate.

—*Robert South*

I SOMETIMES THINK WE EXPECT TOO MUCH of Christmas Day. We try to crowd into it the long arrears of kindliness and humanity of the whole year. As for me, I like to take my Christmas a little at a time, all through the year.

—*David Grayson*

CHRISTMAS! 'TIS THE SEASON for kindling the fire of hospitality in the hall, the genial fire of charity in the heart.

—*Washington Irving*

DESPITE THE FLURRY OF GIFT giving during this time of the year, we already have the most precious gift of all—the presence of the Holy Spirit within our lives.

—*Anonymous*

Reference Notes

Section 2

1. Dietrich Bonhoeffer, *Life Together,* trans. by John W. Doberstein (New York: Harper and Row, 1954), 99.

2. Walter Russell Bowie, *The Interpreter's Bible,* Vol. 8: Luke-John (Nashville: Abingdon, 1980), 62.

3. Donald Goergen, *The Sexual Celibate* (New York: Seabury Press, 1974), 25-6.

Section 3

1. "The Christian Message Today," *Herald of Holiness,* Vol. 33, December 11, 1944, 3.